I0149359

Copyright © 2024-2025 by Pippa Bird

All rights reserved. No part of this book may be reproduced or transmitted in any form or by any means, electronic or mechanical, including photocopying, recording, or by any information storage and retrieval system, without permission in writing from the publisher.

ISBN: 9781764274579

First Edition

Curious Curlew

Feathers and Feelings

Pippa Bird

Curtis believed feelings were like feathers: delicate, powerful,
and filled with curiosity. Each feather held a question - not an answer.

Today, he was following a trail - not of footprints, but of feelings.
His friends needed help, and Curtis knew just how to ask.

Curtis found Bella Bilby curled beneath a
bottlebrush bloom, her ears twitching.

"I feel fluttery," she whispered. "Like something's wrong, but I don't know what."

Curtis stood beside her and pulled a feather from his wing.
He offered the feather and said. "This is sure to help."

"It's just a feather," said the Bilby.
"But it's my feather...and I'm curious."

"I don't understand," sighed Bella.

"I think what you're feeling, is worry," started Curtis, "I'm curious. What does it feel like in your body?"

Bella touched her belly. "It's like butterflies. But not the nice kind."

Curtis nodded. "I'm curious. What do you think the butterflies want you to know?"

Bella thought. "Maybe... that I need a quiet place."

Curtis gave her a seed pod along with the feather.
"Hold this when the fluttering comes.
It reminds you: you're safe, and I'm near."

Curtis heard stomping coming from the small waterhole. Warren was grumbling to himself, his fur bristled, his brow furrowed.

The curlew moved closer, perching himself on a nearby rock. He looked at Warren inquisitively, not uttering a single word.

"I'm not mad!" huffed the wombat. "I just... I don't know what I am!"

Curtis didn't flinch. He offered a
feather and said:
"I believe you're feeling frustration.
And I'm curious. What is this feeling
protecting?"

Warren sat down, thinking for a moment. "Maybe... I'm tired. Maybe I don't want to be strong today."

Curtis the bush stone-curlew nodded.
"What would happen if you let yourself
rest?"

Curtis gave the wombat a bottlebrush bloom along with the feather. "Hold these close," he said.

"Now close your eyes and breathe with me. In... out... Let's rest together a moment."

Curtis found Goldie curled up on the bush floor, silent beneath a fern.

He held out a pale blue feather:
"Sadness.." he started.

"No, Curtis. It feels more complicated
than sadness," said the goanna.

"I'm curious. What memory is this feeling holding?" asked the curlew.

Goldie peeked out. "I miss someone. I miss the way things used to be. Some days it feels too heavy to carry."

Curtis offered a feather along with a scented eucalyptus twig and a stalk of lavender. "I believe you're feeling grief. Grief can be heavy."

Goldie held the bundle close.
"It smells like comfort."

"Let's remember them together.
You're not alone."

As the sun dipped low, Curtis gathered his friends in the bush.
Each held their feather bundle.

They didn't rush to feel better. They asked questions. They listened.
They let the bush hold their stories while they
all held space for each others feelings.

Curtis smiled. "Feelings are like
feathers. Delicate, powerful and
filled with curiosity."

Calm Kangaroo series by Pippa Bird. Available on Amazon.

Calm Kangaroo — Mindfulness Alphabet — Written & Illustrated by Pippa Bird

Quiet Quokka — Written & Illustrated by Pippa Bird

Positive Platypus — Soula's Self-image

Co-regulating Koala — Lost and Found

Unwind with Calm Kangaroo — Written & Illustrated by Pippa Bird

Positive Platypus — Posy's Special Find — Written & Illustrated by Pippa Bird

Co-regulating Koala — Tumbling Tower — Written & Illustrated by Pippa Bird

Co-regulating Koala — The Loud Crack — Written & Illustrated by Pippa Bird

Wobbly Roo — Pippa Bird

Logical Lyrebird — Pippa Bird

Hop by Hop — Pippa Bird — A Gentle Approach to Autism Screening

Hop, Skip, Rest — Pippa Bird — A Gentle Approach to Understanding ADHD

Elated Emu — Pippa Bird

Corroborate Cockatoo — Pippa Bird

Kind Kookaburra — Pippa Bird

Timely Tarantula — Pippa Bird

Nonsense Numbat — Pippa Bird

Polite Python — Pippa Bird

Bully Bilby — Pippa Bird — EXTENDED EDITION

Empathetic Echidna — Pippa Bird

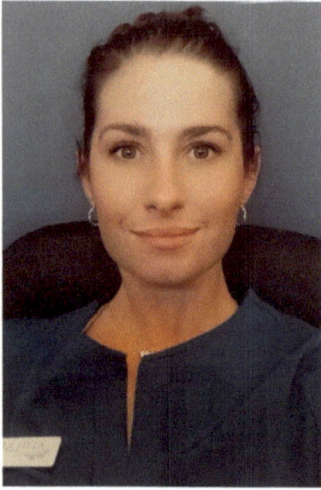

About the Author

Pippa Bird is a former Mental Health Therapist in Private Practice Alula Blu Counselling Services, in regional NSW

Pippa holds a Bachelor in Psychology, a Diploma in Counselling, and a Diploma in Graphic Design, with a primary focus on illustration.

Calm Kangaroo

CALM KANGAROO is a backronym title for a children's mental and emotional well-being program. An initiative designed to educate children about mental health and foster a learning journey of emotional intelligence, resilience and cultivate an open mind through the benefits of reading well-being books, leading to the most important discussions and ideas.

CALM KANGAROO focuses on Curating, Advocating & Leading Mindfulness, & its mission to Kindle Awareness, Nurture Growth, Amplify Resilience, & Orchestrate Open-minds.

www.ingramcontent.com/pod-product-compliance
Lightning Source LLC
LaVergne TN
LVHW072112070426
835509LV00003B/128